GOOD FOOD

Recipes That Keep Them Coming Back

by

Shelley Garrett

Copyright ©2016 Shelley Garrett
All rights reserved.
Printed in the United States of America.
ISBN: 1530317649
ISBN-13: 978-1530317646

DEDICATION

It is with profound gratitude that I dedicate this book to Miss LaReta at the Kaufman County Childen's Shelter. She is saving lives one child at a time.

Lana~

I love, love, love you!

Happy cooking, and remember:

Life's too short to eat margarine.

Be happy & do good.

Ecc. 3:12

♡ Shelley Harrett

One hundred percent of author proceeds from the sale of this book will go to feed the children at the emergency shelter.

FOREWORD

It may be said that families build their own unique cultures around food. There are dishes everyone connects with comfort. Others that are strictly fun—for the big game or July the Fourth. Hurry-up favorites that take advantage of shortcuts to get meals on the table fast. But so many times the good ones come from Aunt Betty or Big Daddy, and everyone in the family is cribbing the recipe.

Shelley Garrett's wonderful benefit collection brings together just such family favorites, anchored in the Texas kitchens of her upbringing and well seasoned with husband Terry's additions. The recipes are proof positive that food doesn't have to be fancy or difficult to make to taste wonderful. And once you've got your sea legs in the galley, so to speak, there's lots of room for experimentation and change-up.

The fact is, convenience products and appliances (love the Crock-Pot®) make tasty cooking easier than ever. And if you say Ro-Tel® (the canned blend of tomatoes and diced green chiles), jalapeños, salsa, chili, okra or Velveeta®, you're talking the language of Texas foods, which is also the language of love at a Texas dinner table.

Kim Pierce

Co-author of *The Phytopia Cookbook* & Dallas food writer

INTRODUCTION

Whether you love to cook or only do it so your family doesn't starve to death, these recipes will appeal to you. They are reliable, delicious and comforting, and for the most part, they are simple and straightforward – chop it, cook it, eat it. If cooking is a joyful meditation for you – enjoy yourself. If cooking is merely tolerable – there are shortcuts and tips to make your life more manageable. No matter what, you are going to be very popular at the potluck.

My only goal for publishing this cookbook is to share my family's favorite food and make the world a tastier place. If you find that you don't have every single ingredient for a recipe, just roll with it. Don't be afraid to substitute rosemary for oregano. Be adventurous. Some of the most amazing culinary treats we've created in our kitchen were lucky improvisations.

I would be remiss if I did not mention that both of my grandmothers were instrumental in my love for cooking. Ma cooked with the greatest of ease – a pinch of this, a pinch of that, and suddenly all 15 provisions were hot and ready at exactly the same time. Nana was pure genius with the peanut grinder and always let us lick the bowl. Her peanut cake and cornbread dressing are legendary. My mom taught me to roll with what you've got on hand and that homegrown tomatoes are way more delicious than the ones you buy at the store. Dad taught me that more is better, and he was right. And finally, my culinary hero is my sweet husband Terry. I greatly admire his precision, patience and persistence with regard to growing Pavuvu peppers, creating his own spice blends and knowing that meat (like people) must rest. God, I love that man.

CONTENTS

STARTERS — 11

- Firecrackers 12
- Fogo Biscuits 13
- Guacamole 14
- Party Pecans 15
- Pizza Dip 16
- Salsa 17
- Shrimp Cocktail 18
- Six-Layer Mexican Dip 19
- Texas Caviar 20
- Tomatillo & Avocado Salsa 21
- Truffled Eggplant 22

SALADS — 23

- Broccoli Ramen Salad 24
- Broccoli Sunshine Salad 25
- Chicken Rotini Salad 26
- Chicken Salad 27
- Corn, Avocado & Tomato Salad 28
- Corn Salad 29
- Must-Go Salad 30
- Pea Salad 31
- Potato Salad 32
- Red Grape & Blue Cheese Chicken Salad 33
- Seven-Layer Salad 34
- Tabouli 35
- Thai Salad 36
- White Bean Salad 37
- Wilted Lettuce Salad 38

SOUPS, CHILIS & STEWS — 39

Baked Potato Soup 40
Black Bean Soup 41
Chicken & Dumplings 42
Chicken Enchilada Soup 43
Chicken Tortilla Soup 44
Cream of Garlic Soup 45
Gumbo 46
Stew 47
Sweet Potato Cauliflower Soup 48
Taco Soup 49
Texas Chili 50
Tomato Basil Soup 51
White Chili 52

SIDES — 53

Bacon Brussels Sprouts 54
Black-Eyed Peas 55
Broccoli Casserole 56
Corn Casserole 57
Dressing 58
Eggplant Stevie Love 59
Green Bean Casserole 60
Hashbrown Casserole 61
Roasted Cabbage 62
Smashed Potatoes 63
Squash Casserole 64

MAINS

- Beef Stroganoff 66
- Breakfast Casserole 67
- Buffalo Chicken Mac 68
- Chicken Carbonara 69
- Chicken Dressing Casserole 70
- Chicken Enchiladas 71
- Chicken Spaghetti 72
- Chicken Tarragon 73
- Crock-Pot® Chicken Olé 74
- Crock-Pot® Meatloaf 75
- Crock-Pot® Roast & Pinto Beans 76
- Eggplant Parmesan Casserole 77
- Fettuccini Alfredo 78
- Goulash 79
- Mexican Chicken Casserole 80
- Pasta Puttanesca 81
- Quiche 82
- Ribs 83
- Seafood Enchiladas 84
- Shrimp Paella 85
- Stuffed Bell Peppers 86
- Tina Beans 87
- Tomato Pie 88

AWESOME SAUCE 89

- Fancy Salad Dressing 90
- Giblet Gravy 91
- Pesto 92
- Poblano Sauce 93
- Sweet & Spicy Mustard Sauce 94

SWEETS 95

- Banana Nut Bread 96
- Banana Pudding (new-fangled) 97
- Banana Pudding (old-fashioned) 98
- Bread Pudding 99
- Buttermilk Pie 100
- Chocolate Chip Pie 101
- Chocolate Chip Pound Cake 102
- Chocolate Meringue Pie 103
- Coconut Cake 104
- Coconut Meringue Pie 105
- Cowboy Cookies 106
- Cream Pie 107
- Depraved Brownies 108
- Easy Fudge 109
- Flourless Chocolate Cake 110
- Fudge Pie 111
- Hello Dollies 112
- Key Lime Pie 113
- Peach Cobbler 114
- Pumpkin Coffee Cake 115
- Pumpkin Pie 116
- Strawberry Cake 117

FIRECRACKERS

- 2 cups canola oil
- 2 oz. dry ranch dressing mix
- 3 tablespoons crushed red pepper
- 2 teaspoons garlic powder
- 1 box saltine crackers

Mix oil, dressing mix and spices in a bowl. Place all four sleeves of crackers in an airtight container. Pour the spicy oil mixture over the crackers. Close the lid on the crackers tightly and flip the container every 5 minutes for about 20 minutes to make sure all crackers got thoroughly coated. The crackers will soak up every bit of the oil.

FOGO BISCUITS

1-½ cups milk

1-½ cups sour tapioca flour

1 cup sweet tapioca flour

¾ cup shredded Parmesan

¾ cup corn oil

4 eggs

1 teaspoon salt

Mix together all ingredients in a large mixing bowl. Spoon liquid batter into a greased mini muffin pan (I use a little ladle), filling each cup only ¾ full because these little gems rise tall and proud like popovers. Bake at 425 degrees for 16 minutes.

GUACAMOLE

2 avocados

2 Roma tomatoes

½ purple onion

1 jalapeño, deseeded

1 bunch cilantro

1 tablespoon pepper sauce

1 teaspoon salt

Pinch of garlic powder

Juice from one lime

If you have a chopper or food processor, cut the vegetables into large chunks, add the seasonings and lime juice, and take it all for a spin in the chopper. If you're dedicated to doing things the old-fashioned way, smash the avocados, finely chop your vegetables, and mix well with the spices and lime juice.

PARTY PECANS

4 tablespoons butter

3 tablespoons sugar

2 tablespoons pepper sauce

1-½ teaspoons salt

½ teaspoon garlic powder

¼ cup whiskey

4 cups pecan halves

Melt butter in saucepan. Add sugar, pepper sauce, salt and garlic powder, and stir over low heat until dissolved. Add whiskey and bring to a boil. Lower heat and simmer for 3 minutes. Stir in the pecans until they are thoroughly coated. Spread the goodness-drenched pecans in a roasting pan or onto a cookie sheet. Bake at 300 degrees for 50 minutes.

All the Garrett men are handy in the kitchen, and our son Travis is no exception. He introduced us to this saucy treat. Borrow a little whiskey from your favorite neighbor and whip up a batch of these in no time.

PIZZA DIP

1 cup pepperoni, chopped

1 cup onion, chopped

1 cup bell pepper, chopped

1 cup black olives, chopped

1 cup green olives, chopped

1 cup mozzarella cheese, shredded

1 cup cheddar cheese, shredded

1 cup mayonnaise

1 teaspoon garlic powder

Mix all ingredients thoroughly and spread into a 9" x 13" baking dish. Bake for 30 minutes at 400 degrees. Serve with any kind of cracker, chip, or toasted bread – or your bare hands.

SALSA

4 Roma tomatoes

6 cloves garlic

½ purple onion

¼ bell pepper

1 jalapeño, deseeded

1 bunch of cilantro

Juice of one lime

Salt to taste

Cut ingredients into chunks and place in a chopper or food processor. Chop to desired fineness, and serve with tortilla chips.

This salsa gives the perfect kick to scrambled eggs, Fettuccini Alfredo, meatloaf, soups and baked potatoes.

SHRIMP COCKTAIL

12 oz. small (71-90) cooked, deveined, tail-off shrimp
12 oz. medium (41-60) cooked, deveined, tail-off shrimp
1 cup spicy Bloody Mary mix
2 avocados, chopped
½ cup sweet onion, chopped
1 small bunch cilantro, finely chopped
1 tablespoon horseradish
1 tablespoon Worcestershire sauce
Juice of two limes, about ⅓ cup
⅓ cup ketchup
1-½ tablespoons hot sauce
Garlic salt to taste
Fresh-cracked pepper to taste

Mix it all up in a huge bowl, and chill for a few hours for maximum flavor percolation. Serve with crackers or chips or nothing at all.

SIX-LAYER MEXICAN DIP

2 cans bean dip
16 oz. guacamole
8 oz. Miracle Whip®
8 oz. sour cream
1.25-oz. envelope taco seasoning
16 oz. picante sauce
1 lb. cheddar cheese, grated
6 green onions, chopped
4 tomatoes, chopped
1 bunch of cilantro, chopped
Garlic salt to taste

Spread bean dip in the bottom of a 9" x 13" casserole dish. Spread guacamole on top of the bean dip. Mix the Miracle Whip, sour cream and taco seasoning, and then spread that mixture on top of the guacamole. Spread the picante sauce on top of the Miracle Whip-sour cream mixture. Add the layer of shredded cheese. Sprinkle onions, tomatoes and cilantro on top of the cheese. Add garlic salt as desired. Serve with tortilla chips.

TEXAS CAVIAR

11-oz. can peg corn, drained

15-oz. can black beans, rinsed & drained

10-oz. can Ro-Tel® tomatoes with liquid

1 bunch of cilantro, chopped

½ purple onion, chopped

2 avocados, chopped

1 teaspoon onion powder

1 teaspoon garlic salt

½ teaspoon Accent® Flavor Enhancer

½ teaspoon black pepper

Mix it all up in a big bowl and refrigerate overnight. Serve with lime-flavored tortilla chips for maximum effect.

TOMATILLO & AVOCADO SALSA

1 lb. tomatillos

1 jalapeño pepper, deseeded

½ bunch cilantro

1 thick slice onion

4 cloves garlic

1 avocado

1-½ teaspoons salt

Purée all ingredients in a blender and refrigerate.

This stuff is good enough to drink (and we have).

Two great blessings came from my husband's ex-wife: Amazing stepchildren and the Texas Caviar recipe. Thanks, Bonnie.

TRUFFLED EGGPLANT

- 2 large eggplants
- 3 oz. prosciutto ham
- 4 oz. goat cheese
- 4 oz. Parmesan, shredded
- Balsamic vinegar
- Truffle oil
- Fresh-cracked pepper

Cut eggplants into ½-inch slices. Lightly salt the slices and let them sweat for about half an hour. Soak up eggplant sweat with paper towels. This process takes away the slightly bitter flavor of the eggplant.

Cook prosciutto in a 350-degree oven for about 10 minutes, or until crispy, and then chop into small pieces. Place eggplant slices onto a greased cookie sheet. Smudge 1-½ teaspoons of goat cheese on each slice of eggplant and then evenly distribute chopped prosciutto on top of the goat cheese. Sprinkle a teaspoon of shredded Parmesan on top of the prosciutto. Drizzle balsamic vinegar over all the slices and bake for 20 minutes in a 350-degree oven. Remove from oven and drip a few drops of truffle oil and some fresh-cracked pepper on each slice before serving.

BROCCOLI RAMEN SALAD

1 pack ramen noodles, broken into pieces

1 cup walnut pieces

1 tablespoon butter

1 head Romaine lettuce, chopped into bite-sized pieces

6 cups broccoli florets, chopped into bite-sized pieces

6 green onions, chopped

DIVINE DRESSING

½ cup olive oil

½ cup sugar

¼ cup red wine vinegar

1-½ tablespoons soy sauce

Salt & pepper to taste

Toast the crushed ramen noodles and walnuts in the butter. Toss all the ingredients in the Divine Dressing, and smile.

Yes, I realize that it is fundamentally wrong to have sugar in salad, but it's so stinking good.

BROCCOLI SUNSHINE SALAD

1 cup mayonnaise

2 tablespoons apple cider vinegar

¼ cup sugar

6 cups broccoli florets, cut into bite-sized pieces

1 cup raisins

1 cup purple onion, chopped

1 cup bacon, crispy & chopped

Mix mayo, vinegar and sugar. Toss all the ingredients with the mayo-vinegar-sugar dressing and let sit overnight in the refrigerator to create a symphony in your mouth.

CHICKEN ROTINI SALAD

- 6 tablespoons red wine vinegar
- 3 tablespoons olive oil
- 1 teaspoon crushed rosemary
- 12-oz. box of wheat rotini noodles
- 2 cups cooked chicken, cubed
- 1 cup walnuts, chopped
- 1 cup carrots, shredded
- ½ cup purple onion, chopped
- 1 cup blue cheese crumbles
- 1 cup grape tomatoes, halved
- 1 cup red seedless grapes, halved
- 2 cups baby spinach
- 1 cup artichoke hearts, chopped

Combine the vinegar, olive oil and rosemary in a blender and set aside. Cook the rotini according to package directions, and drain well. In a large mixing bowl, toss the rotini and all the other ingredients with the dressing. Refrigerate for a couple of hours for infusion perfection.

CHICKEN SALAD

2 cups cooked chicken, chopped

½ cup sliced almonds

½ cup celery, sliced

½ cup carrots, shredded

½ cup green onions, chopped

1 cup mayonnaise or Miracle Whip®

1 teaspoon ground cumin

1 teaspoon dill weed

1 teaspoon garlic salt

1 teaspoon lemon juice

Toss all the ingredients and chill for a couple of hours. Light and lovely.

This is Treska Puckett's take on an old favorite.
It is light and refreshing, just like she is.

CORN, AVOCADO & TOMATO SALAD

4 fresh ears corn, grilled

2 avocados, cubed

1 pint cherry tomatoes, cut in half

½ cup purple onion, finely diced

DRESSING

4 tablespoons olive oil

1 tablespoon lime zest

½ teaspoon sea salt

2 tablespoons fresh lime juice

1 small bunch cilantro, chopped

½ teaspoon pepper

Mix up the dressing in a blender and set aside. Cut the grilled corn off the cob and place in a large mixing bowl. Add the avocado, tomatoes and onion, and toss in the dressing. Refrigerate for a couple of hours for flavor fusion. Super fresh and zingy.

CORN SALAD

2 (15.25-oz.) cans whole kernel corn, drained

½ cup red bell pepper, chopped

½ cup purple onion, chopped

2 cups cheddar cheese, shredded

1 cup mayonnaise

4 cups Chili Cheese Frito® corn chips, crushed

Mix the first five ingredients and chill in the refrigerator. Stir in the corn chips right before serving. I get excited just thinking about eating this stuff.

First, Debbie Knight introduced us to the most amazing sweet treat in human history (fudge pie), and then she ruined us with this salty deliciousness.

MUST-GO SALAD

PANTRY

Black olives	Artichoke hearts	Beans	Beets
Dried fruits	Canned chicken	Capers	Corn
Pasta	Hearts of palm	Mandarin oranges	Nuts
	Peaches	Seeds	

FRIDGE

Basil	Apple	Avocado	Bacon
Garlic	Bell pepper	Cheese	Cucumber
Spinach	Mushrooms	Onion	Quinoa
	Strawberries	Tomatoes	

Every Sunday, we have Must-Go Salad. Depending on what stray ingredients are left in the refrigerator from the prior week, we mix everything into a big salad – because all the scraps must go! Choose any 5 or 6 ingredients in any quantity from the lists. Chop everything into bite-sized pieces, and toss in salad dressing. See Fancy Salad Dressing on page 90. Voilà – Must-Go Salad!

PEA SALAD

2 (15-oz.) cans Le Sueur® very young small sweet peas with mushrooms & pearl onions, drained
¼ cup sweet pickle relish
¼ cup dill pickle relish
½ cup cheddar cheese, shredded
2 boiled eggs, chopped
4-oz. jar of pimentos, drained
½ cup Miracle Whip®
½ cup frozen peas (to add bright green color)

Mix all the ingredients and refrigerate. This is my favorite food on the planet.

I know my grandmother would forgive me for all the shortcuts I take with her recipe. I use relish instead of chopped pickles and shredded cheddar instead of tiny chopped cubes. I know Ma's pea salad is all the rage in heaven.

POTATO SALAD

- 2 lbs. small red potatoes
- 4 boiled eggs, diced
- 2 ribs celery, diced
- ½ cup purple onion, diced
- 4 green onions, sliced
- ½ cup dill pickle, diced
- ¼ cup sour cream
- ¾ cup mayonnaise
- 1 tablespoon vinegar
- 1 tablespoon dill
- 2 teaspoons Dijon mustard
- Salt & pepper to taste

Cut potatoes into bite-sized chunks and boil for 10-12 minutes, until tender. Combine all ingredients and chill.

Sometimes I'm feeling frisky and add a cup of frozen peas or a teaspoon of dried thyme to my potato salad. Adding crispy bacon (to anything) is always a good idea.

RED GRAPE & BLUE CHEESE CHICKEN SALAD

⅓ cup mayonnaise

1-½ tablespoons white wine vinegar

3 oz. crumbled blue cheese

2 (12.5-oz.) cans chunk chicken, drained

1 cup red grapes, cut in half

1 cup green grapes, cut in half

2 celery ribs, thinly sliced

3 tablespoons parsley, chopped

¼ cup walnuts, chopped

Salt & pepper to taste

Mix all ingredients in a large bowl. Refrigerate overnight for maximum taste sensation.

SEVEN-LAYER SALAD

2 heads iceberg lettuce, shredded
1 bag baby spinach, chopped
8 boiled eggs, chopped
1 lb. bacon, cooked crispy & chopped

2 cups tomatoes, chopped
1 bunch green onions, sliced
8 oz. cheddar cheese, grated
10 oz. frozen peas, thawed

DRESSING

1 cup mayonnaise
2 oz. dry ranch dressing mix

1 cup sour cream

In a glass trifle bowl, layer ingredients as follows: iceberg, spinach, eggs, bacon, tomatoes, green onions, cheese and peas. Mix up the dressing and layer on top of the peas, spreading the dressing to the edges of the bowl. Sprinkle with dill and smile. Cover and refrigerate until ready to eat.

We only trust my Aunt Jean to bring this salad and the broccoli casserole to holiday gatherings. You cannot leave the necessities to chance.

TABOULI

1 cup Bob's Red Mill® bulgur wheat

1-½ cups warm water

2 cups parsley, chopped

½ cup green onions, thinly sliced

2 large tomatoes, finely chopped

3 tablespoons fresh mint, finely chopped

½ cup lemon juice

½ cup canola oil

1 can garbanzo beans, rinsed & drained

1 tablespoon Cavender's® All-Purpose Greek Seasoning

Sea salt & pepper to taste

Soak bulgur wheat in warm water for an hour. Drain the bulgur. In a mixing bowl, toss the bulgur wheat with all the other ingredients until thoroughly combined. Refrigerate overnight if possible. Greek greatness.

THAI SALAD

2 cups cooked chicken, chopped

2 cups fresh baby spinach, chopped

1 cup broccoli slaw

4 cloves garlic, minced

1 red bell pepper, chopped

1 bunch cilantro, chopped

1 cucumber, deseeded & chopped

1 tablespoon fresh ginger, minced

¼ cup fresh basil, chopped

⅓ cup cashews, chopped

½ cup sesame ginger salad dressing

In a large mixing bowl, combine all the ingredients and toss in the sesame ginger salad dressing. Yummy freshness.

WHITE BEAN SALAD

1 can white beans, rinsed & drained

1 red pepper, finely chopped

2 cups grape tomatoes, cut in half

6 green onions, sliced

½ cup chopped basil or 2 tablespoons pesto

3.8-oz. can sliced black olives, drained

1 tablespoon olive oil

1 tablespoon white balsamic vinegar

Combine all the ingredients and refrigerate overnight so that all the flavors mingle and get to know each other. This light and refreshing salad is a summertime potluck favorite.

Depending on what I have on hand, I have substituted black beans for white beans and added crumbled feta, chopped avocado and whatever else needed to exit the crisper.

WILTED LETTUCE SALAD

6 slices bacon
1 head fresh leaf lettuce
5 oz. mushrooms, sliced
1 bunch radishes, sliced
3 boiled eggs, sliced
Juice of ½ lemon

¼ cup sugar
2 cloves garlic, minced
¼ cup apple cider vinegar
½ teaspoon salt
½ teaspoon pepper

Fry the bacon extra crispy and save the grease. Tear the lettuce into pieces and place in a glass bowl with the mushrooms, radishes and eggs. Pour the lemon juice over the vegetables, and add the crumbled bacon. To make the dressing, heat the sugar and garlic in the bacon grease in a skillet on the stove. When the sugar is dissolved, add the vinegar, salt and pepper. Bring the dressing to a boil and then pour over the salad and toss. This deliciousness must be eaten immediately.

Maybe it's a Big Daddy thing, but I'm noticing that many of our family favorites contain bacon grease and sugar.

SOUPS, CHILIS & STEWS

BAKED POTATO SOUP

5 lbs. potatoes, cubed
1 large onion, diced
½ cup garlic, minced

1 tablespoon seasoned salt
64 oz. chicken broth
16 oz. cream cheese

FIXINGS

Cheddar cheese, shredded
Green onions, sliced

Bacon, crispy & chopped

Cut the potatoes into quarters and place in the slow cooker with onion, garlic, seasoned salt and broth. Cook on high for 4 hours. Cut the cream cheese into chunks and add to the slow cooker. Stir until cream cheese is melted. Purée with a hand immersion blender until potatoes and cheese are well incorporated and creamy smooth. Garnish with Fixings.

BLACK BEAN SOUP

12 oz. dried black beans
8 cups chicken broth
2 teaspoons olive oil
1 medium onion, chopped
1 cup carrots, chopped
1 cup celery, chopped
2 cloves garlic, minced

2 teaspoons dried oregano
1 teaspoon dried thyme
1 bay leaf
½ teaspoon cayenne pepper
3 tablespoons fresh lime juice
1 bunch cilantro, chopped

Cook black beans with chicken broth in a slow cooker on high for 8 hours. In a large skillet, sauté in olive oil the onion, carrots, celery and garlic until the onion is translucent. Add the sautéed vegetables to the slow cooker with the oregano, thyme, bay leaf and cayenne pepper. Cook for 4 more hours. Purée to desired thickness with a hand immersion blender. Add the lime juice and cilantro just before serving.

Take a hot, steaming vat of this soup to share with your co-workers and suddenly they forget all about that thing you screwed up last week.

CHICKEN & DUMPLINGS

96 oz. chicken broth

3 cans biscuits, cut into quarters

Pint of half & half

6 cups cooked chicken, cubed

1 teaspoon salt

1 teaspoon pepper

Bring broth to a boil in a large stockpot. Slowly drop biscuit dough quarters into the boiling broth. Reduce the heat to medium and stir occasionally for about 5 minutes – if you stir too much, the dumplings disappear. Return the heat to high and add the half & half. When the broth begins to boil again, add the chicken, salt and pepper. Simmer and serve.

CHICKEN ENCHILADA SOUP

1 onion, chopped
2 cloves garlic, minced
1 tablespoon vegetable oil
32 oz. chicken broth
2 cups water
1 cup masa harina
10-oz. can enchilada sauce
2 cups cheddar cheese, shredded
1 teaspoon salt
1 teaspoon chili powder
½ teaspoon cumin
1 lb. cooked rotisserie chicken, de-boned & chopped

In a large stew pot, cook the onion and garlic in oil until the onion is translucent. Add the chicken broth. In a bowl, mix 2 cups of water with the masa harina until well blended. Pour masa into the pot with the broth. Add the enchilada sauce, cheese and spices. Bring to a boil. Add the chopped chicken, and simmer on low heat for 30 minutes so the flavors can fuse.

CHICKEN TORTILLA SOUP

½ cup onion, chopped
3 cloves garlic, chopped
1 green pepper, deseeded & chopped
1 tablespoon canola oil
4 cups chicken broth
15-oz. can tomato sauce
½ tablespoon red pepper flakes

1 teaspoon dried basil
1 bunch cilantro, chopped
2 cups cooked chicken, chopped
1 teaspoon cumin
½ teaspoon salt
1 teaspoon lime juice

Sauté the onion, garlic and green pepper in the oil until the onion is translucent. In a stockpot, bring to a boil the broth and tomato sauce. Add the sautéed onion, garlic, green pepper and all the other ingredients to the stockpot and bring to a boil. Lower the heat and allow to simmer for 30 minutes.

With tortilla soup, the garnish is mandatory, so be sure to fry some strips of corn tortilla, chop an avocado, and have some shredded cheese, sour cream and pico de gallo nearby.

CREAM OF GARLIC SOUP

1-½ sticks butter
1 cup garlic, chopped
1 large yellow onion, chopped
½ cup flour
32 oz. chicken broth
¾ cup heavy whipping cream
1 teaspoon salt
¼ teaspoon cayenne pepper

In a large saucepan, melt the butter and sauté the garlic and onion until translucent and starting to brown. Stir in the flour to form a paste, but do not let the flour turn brown. Add the chicken broth, heavy whipping cream, salt and cayenne, and bring to a boil. Reduce heat and simmer for 30 minutes. Use an immersion blender to make the soup creamy smooth. (You can make creamy soups of all kinds by replacing the cup of garlic with red bell pepper or butternut squash or beans or just about anything.)

GUMBO

¾ cup vegetable oil
1 cup instant roux
2 green peppers, chopped
1 head celery, chopped
2 large onions, chopped
4 cloves garlic, chopped
3 quarts water
8 tablespoons chicken bouillon
2 lbs. shrimp (31-46 weight), peeled, deveined & tail-off
3 (28-oz.) cans tomatoes
1 lb. summer sausage, sliced
2 lbs. okra, sliced frozen
1 tablespoon salt
2 teaspoons basil
1 tablespoon Creole spice
1 tablespoon pepper
3 tablespoons thyme
2 teaspoons oregano
4 bay leaves
2 tablespoons Worcestershire
12 green onions, sliced
½ bunch parsley, chopped
1 lb. crab meat
Rice or quinoa

Heat oil in a cast iron skillet. Add roux, stirring constantly, until dark brown. In a very large stockpot, combine the roux with the green pepper, celery, onion and garlic. Cover and cook over medium heat for 20 minutes, stirring regularly. Add the water, chicken bouillon, tomatoes, sausage, okra and seasonings to the pot. Bring to a boil, and then lower heat and allow to simmer for 1 hour. Add green onion, parsley, shrimp and crab, and simmer for 30 more minutes. Serve over rice or quinoa.

STEW

- 6 oz. large elbow macaroni noodles
- 1 onion, chopped
- 32-oz. pkg. frozen mixed vegetables
- 29-oz. can tomato sauce
- ½ cup sugar
- 2 lbs. roasted chicken, deboned & chopped
- 20-oz. pkg. frozen okra
- 15.25-oz. can whole kernel corn with juice
- 10-oz. can Ro-Tel® tomatoes, not drained
- Salt & pepper to taste

Place all ingredients into a large stewpot (no need to pre-cook the noodles). Fill the empty tomato sauce can with water twice and pour into the stewpot (about 58 oz.). Bring to a boil, stirring regularly, and then simmer on low for one hour. Splash some hot sauce on top and serve with cornbread (and butter, of course).

Mom's Stew was how we knew winter had arrived. For an awesome bit of zing, add a half cup of steak sauce, but don't tell my mom I said that.

SWEET POTATO CAULIFLOWER SOUP

1 large head cauliflower, cut into bite-sized pieces

Olive oil for drizzling

3 medium sweet potatoes, cut into 1-inch pieces

1 sweet onion, diced

6 cloves garlic

½ teaspoon salt

3 cups chicken broth

¼ teaspoon garam masala

Place cauliflower on a cookie sheet. Drizzle the cauliflower with olive oil, and bake at 400 degrees for 30 minutes, until golden brown. In a stockpot, boil the sweet potatoes, onion and garlic with the salt and chicken broth until tender. Add the cauliflower and garam masala to the stockpot and purée with an immersion hand blender.

Garam masala is a blend of spices often used in Indian dishes. Go ahead and buy a jar from the spice aisle – it's delicious on roasted chicken and grilled fish, too.

TACO SOUP

6 green onions, sliced

3 cloves garlic, minced

16-oz. can pinto beans, rinsed & drained

15-oz. can black beans, rinsed & drained

3 cups cooked chicken, chopped (or 1 lb. cooked ground beef)

15.25-oz. can whole kernel corn, drained

2 (10-oz.) cans Ro-Tel® tomatoes (I use one regular & one spicy)

15-oz. can tomato sauce

14.5-oz. can chicken broth

1.25-oz. pkg. taco seasoning

1 oz. dry ranch dressing mix

Dump all the ingredients into a slow cooker on high for 2 hours. Cilantro, sour cream and shredded cheese are excellent accouterments served on top of a piping hot bowl of this easy soup.

TEXAS CHILI

- 1 lb. bacon, cut into pieces
- 1 large onion, chopped
- 10 cloves garlic, crushed
- 7-oz. can diced green chiles, drained
- 2 poblanos, deseeded & chopped
- 2 jalapeños, deseeded & chopped
- 2 lbs. ground beef
- 1 lb. ground sausage
- 15-oz. can tomato sauce
- 10-oz. can Ro-Tel® tomatoes
- 1 tablespoon vinegar
- 1 tablespoon Worcestershire
- 1 small square dark chocolate
- ¼ cup chili powder
- 1-½ teaspoon salt
- 1 teaspoon cinnamon
- 1 teaspoon cumin
- 1 teaspoon black pepper
- Dash of allspice

Cook the bacon extra crispy, and set aside. Sauté onions, garlic, chiles, poblanos and jalapeños in a little bacon grease until lightly browned. Brown the beef and sausage, and drain the grease. In a large stockpot, combine the sautéed vegetables, browned beef, sausage, bacon, tomato sauce, Ro-Tel and all others ingredients. Fill the tomato sauce can (15 oz.) with water and add to pot. Simmer for 1 hour.

Chili leftovers are as good as the original rodeo. Nothing is more tasty than Frito® chili pie, tacos and tostada salads with Texas Chili leftovers.

TOMATO BASIL SOUP

4 cups tomatoes, chopped

3 cups tomato juice

1 cup chicken broth

12 to 14 fresh basil leaves

1 cup heavy whipping cream

1 stick butter

Salt & pepper to taste

Combine tomatoes, juice and broth in a saucepan on the stove and simmer for 30 minutes. Add basil leaves to the saucepan and purée with an immersion hand blender. Add the cream and butter and stir over low heat until melted and thoroughly combined.

WHITE CHILI

4-oz. can chopped green chiles, drained
1 jalapeño, deseeded & chopped
1 medium white onion, chopped
¼ cup garlic, minced
2 tablespoons vegetable oil
2 (12.5-oz.) cans chicken breast, drained
2 cans great northern beans, rinsed & drained
14-½ oz. can chicken broth

1 cup sour cream
1 tablespoon ground cumin
1 teaspoon oregano
1 teaspoon black pepper
1 teaspoon cayenne pepper
1 teaspoon salt
1 teaspoon dried cilantro

Sauté chiles, jalapeño, onion and garlic in the vegetable oil. In a stockpot, combine sautéed onions and peppers with the chicken, beans, broth, sour cream and all other ingredients. Bring to a boil, and then lower the heat to simmer for 1 hour. For extra creaminess, purée one of the cans of beans in the blender with a little of the chicken broth and return to the stockpot. This is a chili cook-off winner!

SIDES

BACON BRUSSELS SPROUTS

12 slices bacon

2 lbs. fresh or frozen Brussels sprouts, halved

1 cup fresh or dried cranberries

3 cloves garlic, minced

½ yellow onion, chopped

2 tablespoons apple cider vinegar

2 teaspoons garlic salt

Cut bacon into 1-inch pieces and fry in a stockpot or large saucepan until extra crispy. Add Brussels sprouts, cranberries, garlic and onion. Cook covered until Brussels are browned and onion is translucent. Fresh Brussels will take longer to get tender. Add vinegar and garlic salt and cook on low, stirring regularly, until all ingredients have caramelized.

BLACK-EYED PEAS

16 oz. dried black-eyed peas

48 oz. chicken broth

16 oz. ham, cubed

13 oz. skinless smoked sausage, sliced into 1-inch slices

1 large white onion, chopped

8 cloves garlic, minced

2 jalapeños, deseeded & chopped

½ teaspoon salt

½ teaspoon cayenne pepper

½ teaspoon thyme

27-oz. can seasoned collard greens, drained

Throw everything but the collard greens into a slow cooker and cook on high for 6 hours. Add the drained can of collard greens and stir well. Cook for 1 more hour on the slow cooker's low setting.

BROCCOLI CASSEROLE

16 oz. frozen chopped broccoli

16 oz. Velveeta®

1 can cream of broccoli soup

1 cup white onion, chopped

1 cup minute rice

4.5-oz. can of green chiles (optional)

Mix all the ingredients in a large mixing bowl. Spread into a greased 9" x 13" casserole dish and bake at 350 degrees for 35 minutes – until bubbly and brown.

If you're feeling adventurous, replace the rice with pre-cooked quinoa. Bite-for-bite, quinoa has five times more potassium, fiber and iron than white rice does. Okay, sermon over.

CORN CASSEROLE

15.25-oz. can whole kernel corn, drained

14.75-oz. can cream corn

4 oz. corn muffin mix

1 cup cheddar cheese, grated

½ cup butter, softened

1 egg

Mix all the ingredients in a large mixing bowl. Pour into a greased 9" x 13" baking dish. Bake at 375 degrees for 45 minutes. Simple and divine.

DRESSING

- 2 chicken thighs & 2 chicken legs
- 1 gallon water
- 1 cup white onion, chopped
- 1 green bell pepper, deseeded & diced
- ½ jar pimentos, drained
- 3 tablespoons sage
- 2 pans cornbread (9-inch round pans), cooked well done
- 2 cans biscuits, cooked
- 1 cup celery, chopped
- 5 eggs (3 boiled, 2 beaten)
- 1-½ tablespoons coarse black pepper
- Salt to taste

Boil the chicken in a large stockpot with a gallon of water to create broth. Tear the chicken into bite-sized pieces and set aside.

Mix the following ingredients by hand in a large mixing bowl: onion, bell pepper, pimentos, sage, cornbread, biscuits, celery, chopped boiled eggs, beaten eggs, black pepper and chicken pieces. Add broth a little at a time, squeezing through the mixture with your hands, until it takes on a liquid-bread consistency.

Pour into a deep casserole dish. Bake at 400 degrees for 30 minutes, and then lower to 350 degrees for another 30 minutes.

This is Nana's notorious dressing. She will only eat it with giblet gravy and the jellied cranberry sauce. I advise you to do the same.

EGGPLANT STEVIE LOVE

1 eggplant, cut into cubes
1 yellow pepper, deseeded & chopped
1 green pepper, deseeded & chopped
1 red bell pepper, deseeded & chopped
1 cup purple onion, chopped
1 cup tomatoes, chopped
10 cloves garlic, minced
2 teaspoons Creole seasoned salt
¼ cup olive oil
½ cup Parmesan, grated

Toss all the ingredients in a large mixing bowl. Spread out on a large baking sheet. Cook for 50 minutes at 350 degrees. Colorful, simple, fresh deliciousness.

GREEN BEAN CASSEROLE

1 cup fresh mushrooms, sliced
½ cup onion, diced
⅓ stick butter
3 cups cooked green beans
1 cup cheddar, grated

1 can cream mushroom soup
½ cup milk
6-oz. can French-fried onions
1 teaspoon pepper
1 teaspoon garlic powder

Sauté the mushrooms and onions in the butter. In a mixing bowl, combine the mushrooms and onions with the green beans, cheese, soup, milk, half of the French-fried onions and spices. Pour into a 1-½ quart baking dish. Sprinkle the other half of the French-fried onions on top. Bake at 350 degrees for 35 minutes.

HASHBROWN CASSEROLE

2 cans cream of chicken soup

30-oz. bag of frozen hash browns, shredded style

1 stick butter, melted

8 oz. sour cream

2 cups cheddar cheese, shredded

1 teaspoon salt

1 teaspoon pepper

Stir together all the ingredients thoroughly in a large mixing bowl. Place in a 9" x 13" baking dish. Bake at 350 degrees for 1 hour and 10 minutes. I have yet to meet a human who does not love this comforting deliciousness. It freezes well, so it's easy to keep a couple on hand for friends who need a food hug.

ROASTED CABBAGE

1 head green or red cabbage

¼ cup lemon juice

¼ cup olive oil

4 teaspoons Worcestershire sauce

4 teaspoons Soy sauce

Salt & pepper

6 slices bacon, crispy & chopped

Cut out the core of the cabbage and then cut into four wedges. Place two large pieces of foil into a baking pan or on top of a cookie sheet. Place the wedges on top of the foil. Drizzle the cabbage quarters with lemon juice, olive oil, Worcestershire and soy sauce. Salt and pepper each wedge, and crumble bacon bits on top of each. Wrap the foil over the top of the cabbage and create a sealed envelope. Bake at 400 degrees for 50 minutes.

Kindly overlook the stinky sulfur smell of cabbage. It is chock full of potassium and fiber, and it's good luck, too.

SMASHED POTATOES

10 small red potatoes

Olive oil

1 teaspoon kosher salt

1 teaspoon fresh-cracked black pepper

1 teaspoon dried basil

1 teaspoon dried thyme

1 teaspoon dried rosemary

Boil the potatoes for 15 minutes or until fork-tender. Strain and set aside. Slather olive oil onto a baking sheet. Lay the potatoes on the baking sheet and smash flat with a heavy spatula or your bare hands. Drizzle more olive oil over the tops of the smashed potatoes. Sprinkle with salt, pepper and the other herbs. Bake at 450 degrees for 30 minutes or until crispy brown.

SQUASH CASSEROLE

2 lbs. yellow squash, cubed

½ cup onion, chopped

6 tablespoons butter

1 cup cheddar cheese, shredded

½ cup Romano cheese, shredded

1 cup sour cream

1 cup crushed corn flakes

1 tablespoon sugar

1 teaspoon salt

Fresh-cracked pepper to taste

Boil squash until tender; press out excess liquid. Cook the onion in butter until translucent. In a mixing bowl, thoroughly combine the squash, onion with butter and remaining ingredients. Pour mixture into a 9" x 13" casserole dish. Bake at 400 degrees for 30 minutes.

BEEF STROGANOFF

- 1-½ lbs. ground beef
- 1 med. onion, chopped
- 12 oz. egg noodles
- 2 cans cream of mushroom soup
- 1 cup sour cream
- 2 teaspoons dill weed
- 2 teaspoons garlic salt
- 1 teaspoon pepper

Brown the beef with the onion in a large skillet. Drain the grease and set meat and onion aside. Cook the egg noodles according to package directions. Rinse the noodles and return to the pan. Add the beef, onion and all remaining ingredients to the noodles. Mix well and stir over low heat for 25 minutes to let the flavors blend.

BREAKFAST CASSEROLE

2 lbs. sausage

2 cups fiesta blend cheese, shredded

6 eggs, beaten

¾ cup milk

Salt & pepper to taste

Brown the sausage and drain well. Mix all ingredients and pour into a 9" x 13" casserole dish. Bake at 425 degrees for 25 minutes. Originally, this recipe called for biscuit dough or tortillas in the bottom of the baking dish, but we cut out the filler because we are serious about the meat.

BUFFALO CHICKEN MAC

12-oz. pkg. mac & cheese dinner
1-½ cups cooked chicken, chopped
2 tablespoons hot wing sauce
½ cup cheddar cheese, shredded
½ cup green onions, sliced

Prepare mac & cheese as directed on package. In a large mixing bowl, combine mac & cheese, chicken, hot wing sauce, cheese and green onion. Bake in a 9" x 9" baking dish at 425 degrees for 20 minutes, until cheese is bubbly and brown.

Our middle son Tyler deemed this comfort food to be cookbook-worthy, and we trust his taste buds implicitly. The Garrett men have culinary genius in their DNA.

CHICKEN CARBONARA

- 12 oz. spaghetti
- 8 slices bacon
- 1 medium onion, chopped
- 2 cloves garlic, minced
- 2 cups cooked chicken, chopped
- ½ cup Parmesan, grated
- ½ cup heavy whipping cream
- 1 teaspoon salt

Cook and drain spaghetti. Cook bacon extra crispy. Cook garlic and onion in 2 tablespoons of bacon grease until onion is translucent. In a large saucepan, combine the spaghetti, bacon, onion, garlic, chicken, Parmesan, cream and salt until heated thoroughly.

CHICKEN DRESSING CASSEROLE

4 cups cooked chicken, chopped

1 can cream of mushroom soup

1 can cream of chicken soup

10.5-oz. can chicken broth

1 cup milk

14 oz. herb-seasoned stuffing

1 stick butter, melted

Mix all ingredients thoroughly and place in a greased 9" x 13" baking dish. Bake at 350 degrees for 35 minutes or until dark brown.

This casserole is the perfect gift for a busy mom or sickly friend. Be sure to include a jar of turkey gravy and a can of cranberry sauce.

CHICKEN ENCHILADAS

1 can cream of chicken soup
½ cup picante sauce
1.25-oz. envelope taco seasoning
8.5-oz. can creamed corn
½ cup sour cream
2 cups cooked chicken, chopped

2 cups Mexican blend cheese, finely shredded
12 corn tortillas
10-oz. can red enchilada sauce
2 tomatoes, chopped
3.8-oz. can sliced black olives, drained
2 green onions, sliced

Mix the soup, picante sauce, taco seasoning, corn, sour cream and chicken with 1 cup of the cheese. Spread about a half cup of mixture into each tortilla, roll it up, and place seam down in a 9" x 13" baking dish. Evenly pour the enchilada sauce over the enchiladas, and sprinkle the other cup of cheese over the top. Bake at 350 degrees for 40 minutes. Top with chopped tomatoes, olives and onions.

CHICKEN SPAGHETTI

2 cups cooked chicken, chopped

1 can cream of chicken soup

1 can cream of mushroom soup

1 cup milk

16 oz. Velveeta® cheese

12 oz. spaghetti noodles

Chopped black olives (optional)

Mix first five ingredients in a saucepan until melted and creamy smooth. Cook the spaghetti according to package directions and drain thoroughly. Toss the boiled spaghetti noodles with the creamy goodness and black olives until thoroughly combined. Pour into a 9" x 13" casserole dish and bake for 30 minutes at 375 degrees.

This dish may be the winner for the most kid-friendly comfort food of all time. Keep a disposable casserole dish of this deliciousness in the freezer to welcome new neighbors and delight exhausted mommy friends.

CHICKEN TARRAGON

4 boneless, skinless chicken breasts or thighs

1 tablespoon olive oil

1 tablespoon butter

3 tablespoons shallot, diced

1 tablespoon dried tarragon

½ cup heavy whipping cream

1 teaspoon fresh lemon juice

¼ teaspoon salt

¼ teaspoon pepper

Pound the chicken to a ½-inch thickness. Sauté the chicken in the olive oil and butter until browned. Remove the chicken from the pan and set aside. Sauté the shallot and tarragon in the excess olive oil and butter. Once the shallot is translucent, add the cream, lemon juice, salt and pepper. Bring to a boil and then add the chicken back to the pan, smothering with the creamy goodness.

CROCK-POT® CHICKEN OLÉ

1 can cream of chicken soup

1 can cream of mushroom soup

10-oz. can green chili enchilada sauce

1 cup sour cream

1 medium onion, chopped

4 cups cooked chicken, chopped

12 corn tortillas

1-½ cups fiesta blend cheese, finely shredded

Mix soups, enchilada sauce, sour cream and chopped onion in a mixing bowl. Lightly grease the bottom and sides of a Crock-Pot. Layer the following: half of the soup mixture, half of the chicken and 6 tortillas; the other half of the soup mixture, the other half of the chicken and 6 tortillas. Cover and cook on low for 4 to 5 hours. Sprinkle cheese on top and cook another 30 minutes, until cheese is melted.

CROCK-POT® MEATLOAF

1 lb. sausage

1 lb. ground beef

1 cup ketchup

1-½ tablespoons barbecue sauce

1 envelope onion soup mix

½ cup dry bread crumbs

2 eggs

1 teaspoon salt

1 teaspoon garlic powder

Combine all the ingredients (reserving ½ cup of ketchup for later) in a large mixing bowl with your hands. Make sure all ingredients are well mixed and shape into the bottom of a Crock-Pot. Cover and cook on low heat for 5 hours. Spread the remaining ½ cup of ketchup on top of the meatloaf. Cover and continue cooking on low for 30 more minutes. Balsamic ketchup is awesome in this recipe, and you're always welcome to add chopped green pepper, cilantro, fresh tomato or mushrooms to the meat.

My dad told me about this one, and if my dad says it's good, it's good.

CROCK-POT® ROAST & PINTO BEANS

2 cups dry pinto beans

10-oz. can Ro-Tel® tomatoes, not drained

1 yellow onion, chopped

6 cups water

1 tablespoon cumin

1 tablespoon garlic salt

1 teaspoon chili powder

3- to 5-lb. chuck roast

Mix everything but the roast in a Crock-Pot. Pan sear all sides of the roast in a red-hot cast iron skillet. Add the roast to the Crock-Pot and cook for 8-10 hours on the high setting.

EGGPLANT PARMESAN CASSEROLE

No-stick cooking spray

2 eggs

2 tablespoons water

1 cup Parmesan cheese, finely grated

1 teaspoon oregano

1 teaspoon basil

1 teaspoon garlic salt

2 eggplants, sliced into ½-inch rounds

2 (24-oz.) cans spaghetti sauce

2 cups mozzarella cheese, shredded

Spray cookie sheet with no-stick cooking spray. Whisk together eggs and water. In another bowl, combine Parmesan and spices. Dip the eggplant slices in the egg mixture and then in the Parmesan mixture. Place the eggplant on the greased cookie sheet and bake for 15 minutes at 375 degrees. Flip the slices and bake for 15 minutes on the other side.

Pour half a can of spaghetti sauce into the bottom of a 9" x 13" baking dish or oblong casserole dish. Place a layer of half of the eggplant, then half a can of spaghetti sauce and half of the mozzarella. Place the remaining eggplant slices, then a full can of spaghetti sauce and the remaining mozzarella. Bake until brown, bubbling and melty…about 40 minutes at 375 degrees.

Eggplants are misunderstood and underused. They contain phyto nutrients that improve blood circulation and nourish the brain, and they're delicious.

FETTUCCINI ALFREDO

12 oz. fettuccini noodles
1 stick butter
½ pint heavy whipping cream
½ cup Parmesan cheese, grated

Cook the noodles according to package directions; drain and set aside. In a large saucepan, melt the butter and add whipping cream until bubbling, and then add Parmesan until creamy and melted. Toss the cooked fettuccini noodles in the Alfredo sauce and be happy.

GOULASH

- 12 oz. elbow macaroni
- 2 lbs. ground beef
- 2 tablespoons olive oil
- 1 cup onion, chopped
- 3 cloves garlic, minced
- 1 tablespoon brown sugar
- 2 teaspoons paprika
- ¾ cup ketchup
- 2 teaspoons salt
- 1 teaspoon ground black pepper
- 2 tablespoons Worcestershire sauce
- 1 cup water
- ½ teaspoon dry mustard

Boil the macaroni according to package directions. Drain noodles and set aside. Brown the ground beef in olive oil with onion and garlic. Drain the beef. In a large saucepan, combine all remaining ingredients and simmer on low for 10 minutes.

MEXICAN CHICKEN CASSEROLE

4 cups cooked chicken, chopped

1 can cream of mushroom soup

1 can cream of chicken soup

2 cups Monterrey Jack cheese, shredded

10-oz. can Ro-Tel® tomatoes

1 onion, chopped

3 cups tortilla chips, crushed

Thoroughly combine all ingredients in a large mixing bowl. Bake at 400 degrees for 35 minutes in a 9" x 13" baking dish.

This dish may be the winner for the most kid-friendly comfort food of all time. Keep a disposable casserole dish of this deliciousness in the freezer to welcome new neighbors and delight exhausted mommy friends.

PASTA PUTTANESCA

1 lb. spaghetti
10 cloves garlic, minced
1 tablespoon anchovy paste
½ teaspoon red pepper flakes
⅓ cup olive oil
½ cup Kalamata olives, pitted
2 tablespoons capers, drained
24-oz. can spaghetti sauce
¾ cup fresh basil, chopped

Cook pasta according to package directions. Drain and set aside. In a large saucepan, cook the garlic, anchovy paste and red pepper in the olive oil until garlic turns golden. Add the olives and capers and sauté for 2 more minutes. Stir in the spaghetti sauce, and bring to a boil. Add the noodles and basil to the sauce and simmer, stirring until noodles are thoroughly coated and warm.

QUICHE

- 12 oz. evaporated milk
- 3 large eggs
- ½ teaspoon dried thyme
- ¼ teaspoon salt
- ¼ teaspoon ground pepper
- 8 oz. jalapeño cheddar, shredded
- ½ cup ham, cubed
- ¼ cup green onions, diced
- 1 unbaked 9-inch deep-dish pie shell

Whisk the milk, eggs, thyme, salt and pepper in a mixing bowl. Add the cheese, ham and green onions, and stir well. Pour into the pie shell, and bake at 350 degrees for 55 minutes.

RIBS

1 rack of pork ribs (about 4 lbs.)

1 cup barbecue sauce

DRY RUB

½ cup brown sugar

1 tablespoon kosher salt

2 tablespoons Tony Chacere's® Original Creole Seasoning

1 tablespoon fresh-cracked pepper

1 tablespoon dry mustard

Rub the ribs thoroughly on all sides with the Dry Rub. Wrap the rack of ribs in heavy-duty saran wrap and then with heavy-duty foil. Bake in the oven for 4 hours at 220 degrees. Take out of the oven and let cool. Refrigerate overnight. Throw the rack of ribs on the grill until marked with grill marks. Brush the ribs with barbecue sauce and close the grill for 20 more minutes to get them gooey and warm.

My husband Terry's ribs and rubs are the best in Texas. He is the meat master of Highland Drive and the love of my life.

SEAFOOD ENCHILADAS

½ cup onion, chopped

1 tablespoon olive oil

1 can cream of chicken soup

¼ teaspoon nutmeg

½ teaspoon salt

½ teaspoon pepper

8 oz. crab meat

2 cups Monterey Jack cheese, shredded

8 white corn tortillas

1 cup milk

Sauté onions in olive oil until translucent. Mix together soup, onion, nutmeg, salt and pepper. In another bowl, mix the crab, 1 cup of cheese and half of the soup mixture. Set aside. Heat tortillas in the microwave for 20 seconds in order to make them pliable. Place soup-crab mixture in each tortilla, roll up, and place seam-side down in a baking dish. Whisk the milk into the reserved soup mixture and pour over the enchiladas. Sprinkle the remaining ¾ cup of cheese on top. Bake at 350 degrees for 35 minutes, until bubbly and brown.

As with pretty much everything we cook at our house, we like to kick it up a notch by adding the heat. Add Hatch chiles or diced jalapeños to the enchilada filling to spice it up.

SHRIMP PAELLA

½ yellow onion, chopped
8 cloves garlic, minced
6 tablespoons butter (separated)
1 pinch saffron
1 tablespoon chicken bouillon
½ cup green pepper, deseeded & chopped
½ cup red pepper, deseeded & chopped
1 tablespoon jalapeño pepper, deseeded & chopped
½ cup black olives, chopped

2 tablespoons capers
2 bay leaves
14.5-oz. can diced tomatoes
½ tablespoon sugar
1-½ lbs. jumbo shrimp, peeled & deveined
4 teaspoons oregano
2 cups instant brown rice
⅓ cup parsley, chopped
⅓ cup cilantro, chopped

In a large pan, sauté the onions and garlic in 4 tablespoons of butter. Add the saffron, bouillon, peppers, olives, capers, bay leaves, diced tomatoes and sugar, and simmer on low heat. In a separate pan, sauté the shrimp with the oregano in the remaining 2 tablespoons of butter until the shrimp whiten. Drain the shrimp, and add to the main pan.

Cook the rice according to package directions. Add the rice to the main pan. Add the parsley and cilantro to the main pan and cook on low heat for 5 minutes, stirring constantly. Turn off the heat and cover the pan. Let sit for 30 minutes before serving.

STUFFED BELL PEPPERS

6 bell peppers
½ cup onion, chopped
6 cloves garlic, minced
2 cups ground beef or quinoa
1 bunch cilantro, chopped
15.25-oz. can whole kernel corn, drained

1 cup Mexican blend cheese, shredded
Salt & pepper to taste
1 teaspoon chili powder
10-oz. can Ro-Tel® tomatoes, drained
15.25-oz. can black beans, drained

Cut the tops off the green peppers, removing the stem, seeds and membranes – set aside. Sauté the onion and garlic with the ground beef until thoroughly cooked and then drain. Mix all the other ingredients with the meat in a large mixing bowl. Stuff the bell peppers with meat mixture and place in baking dish. Bake at 350 degrees for 35 minutes.

TINA BEANS

- 1 lb. regular sausage, cooked & drained
- 1 lb. hot sausage, cooked & drained
- 1 lb. bacon, crisp & finely chopped
- 2 (53-oz.) cans pork & beans, drain one can
- 2 shots whiskey
- 28-oz. bottle Honey BBQ sauce
- 10-oz. can hot Ro-Tel® tomatoes, drained
- 10-oz. can original Ro-Tel® tomatoes, drained
- 1 cup brown sugar
- ¾ cup honey
- 4-oz. can chopped jalapeños with juice

In a large stockpot, combine all the ingredients and bring to a boil. Lower heat and simmer on low heat until all flavors percolate (about 1 hour).

My dad brought this meaty marvel into our lives.
God bless you, Tina…whoever you are.

TOMATO PIE

- ½ teaspoon salt
- 4 fresh tomatoes, sliced
- 1 tablespoon milk
- 9-inch unbaked deep-dish pie crust
- 10-12 leaves fresh basil, chopped
- ⅓ cup mayonnaise
- ⅓ cup mozzarella cheese, shredded
- ⅓ cup Parmesan cheese, shredded
- 1 clove garlic, minced
- Salt & pepper

Salt the tomato slices and place on paper towels for about 10 minutes. Press the tops of the tomatoes with paper towels to absorb the excess moisture. Brush milk on the pie shell and bake at 450 degrees for 5 minutes. Fill the baked pie crust with tomato slices and sprinkle with the basil. In a mixing bowl, combine the mayo, cheeses, garlic, salt and pepper. Spread the cheese mixture over the tomatoes and basil, spreading to the edges of the pie crust. Bake at 350 degrees for 50 minutes.

AWESOME SAUCE

FANCY SALAD DRESSING

½ cup balsamic vinegar

½ cup olive oil

1 tablespoon Worcestershire sauce

1 tablespoon lemon juice

1 tablespoon garlic, minced

2 teaspoons Dijon mustard

Mix it all up in the blender. Introduce to a nice salad.

Two other quickie salad dressings I whip up in the blender are as follows: (1) ½ cup balsamic vinegar, ½ cup olive oil and 2 tablespoons of pesto; and (2) ½ cup olive oil, 2 tomatoes, 1 onion, 3 cloves garlic and 1 tablespoon lemon juice.

GIBLET GRAVY

- 3 tablespoons butter
- 3 tablespoons flour
- 3 cups chicken or turkey broth
- Giblets & turkey neck, finely chopped
- 1 teaspoon salt
- ½ teaspoon black pepper
- 2 boiled eggs, chopped

Melt the butter in a saucepan. Add the flour, stirring constantly, until smooth and dissolved. Stir in the broth, chopped giblets & neck, salt and pepper, and bring to a boil. Reduce heat and simmer, stirring occasionally, until giblets are cooked and gravy has thickened. Stir in the chopped eggs just before serving.

PESTO

3 cups packed fresh basil leaves

4 cloves garlic

¾ cup Parmesan cheese, grated

½ cup olive oil

¼ cup pine nuts

Combine all ingredients in a food processor. Blend to a smooth paste. Pesto is perfect on pasta, chicken and fish, and the perfect base for salad dressings, too.

POBLANO SAUCE

1 small yellow onion, finely chopped

2 ears corn, grilled & cut off the cob

1 large poblano pepper, roasted, deseeded & chopped

1 large tomato, chopped

3 tablespoons butter

½ cup crème fraîche or drained sour cream

½ cup Monterrey Jack cheese, shredded

1 small bunch cilantro, chopped

1 teaspoon salt

1 tablespoon lime juice

In a large saucepan, sauté the onion, corn, pepper and tomato in the butter until the onion is translucent. Add the crème fraîche and cheese and stir over low heat until completely melted. Add the cilantro, salt and lime juice, and stir until thoroughly combined.

This sauce is particularly amazing on grilled chicken but would probably make a dirty old boot taste delicious. Use 4 ears of corn and serve as a side dish.

SWEET & SPICY MUSTARD SAUCE

1 cup malt vinegar

6 oz. mustard powder

2 egg yolks

1 cup sugar

Mix vinegar and mustard powder and let stand overnight. Mix egg yolks and sugar with vinegar mustard mixture with an electric mixer or blender for 1 minute. Place in a double boiler for 20 minutes, stirring often.

Erika Crump taught me this one, and now we can't eat spiral ham without it. This is also delicious with hot links and kielbasa.

SWEETS

BANANA NUT BREAD

1-1/3 cups flour

1 cup sugar

1/3 cup butter, melted

2 eggs

1 teaspoon vanilla extract

1/2 teaspoon ginger

1-1/2 cups overly ripe bananas (4 or 5), mashed

1/2 cup pecans, chopped

1/3 cup water

1 teaspoon baking soda

1/2 teaspoon salt

1/4 teaspoon baking powder

Mix all ingredients in a mixing bowl with a hand mixer. Pour into a greased loaf pan and bake at 350 degrees for 60 minutes. Serve it hot with real butter or don't serve it at all. And be sure to make French toast with it on Saturday morning.

BANANA PUDDING (NEW-FANGLED)

2 small boxes instant banana cream pudding (requires milk)
14-oz. can sweetened condensed milk
4 oz. Cool Whip®
Box vanilla wafers
4 bananas

Prepare banana cream pudding per "pie filling" instructions on the box. Mix the pie filling, sweetened condensed milk and Cool Whip with a hand mixer until creamy smooth. In a 2-quart dish, layer vanilla wafers, half of the pudding and then all four bananas cut into 1-inch slices. Add the rest of the pudding on top of the banana slices and finish with a layer of vanilla wafers on top. Refrigerate.

My mom refuses to call this banana pudding because she's old school, but this new-fangled concoction certainly has its charms. See the old-fashioned version for Mom's classic.

BANANA PUDDING (OLD-FASHIONED)

1 cup sugar
2 tablespoons flour
¼ teaspoon salt
2 cups milk

2 eggs
1 teaspoon vanilla extract
Box vanilla wafers
4 bananas

In saucepan over medium heat, combine sugar, flour, salt, milk and eggs. Stir continually until thickened. After it's good and thick, remove from heat and add vanilla. In a 2-quart dish, layer vanilla wafers, half of the pudding and then all four bananas cut into 1-inch slices. Add the rest of the pudding on top of the banana slices and finish with a layer of vanilla wafers on top. This is delicious warm or cold.

BREAD PUDDING

2 small loaves raisin cinnamon bread
2 cups milk
6 eggs

1 tablespoon vanilla
2 cups sugar
¼ teaspoon salt

1 stick butter

BRANDY SAUCE

1 cup sugar   1 stick butter, melted   1 teaspoon brandy or rum   ½ pint whipping cream

Tear the raisin bread into pieces and place in a large mixing bowl. Add the milk, eggs and vanilla and stir thoroughly. Add the sugar and salt, and stir some more. Place the bread pudding mixture into a greased 9" x 13" baking dish. Cut the stick of butter into ½-inch pats and dot the top of the bread pudding mixture. Bake for 30 minutes at 350 degrees. Remove from oven and stir thoroughly. Return pan to oven and bake for 30 more minutes.

Mix the Brandy Sauce in a blender and pour over the bread pudding when you take it out of the oven. Let sit for 5 minutes before serving. Thank goodness Prissy shared this recipe with us! It makes momma very happy.

BUTTERMILK PIE

1-½ cups sugar

½ cup flour

3 eggs

½ cup buttermilk

¾ cup butter, soft from setting out (do not melt)

½ teaspoon vanilla

9-inch deep-dish pie shell

Mix ingredients with hand mixer for at least 2 minutes. Pour into the unbaked pie shell. Bake for one hour and 15 minutes at 325 degrees.

If you're going to bake one Buttermilk Pie, you might as well bake two and make an unsuspecting friend very happy. This is the only foolproof way we can get our daughter Rylie to come visit us.

CHOCOLATE CHIP PIE

2 eggs
½ cup sugar
½ cup brown sugar
½ cup flour
1-½ sticks butter, softened
1 cup chocolate chips
1 cup chopped pecans
9-inch deep-dish pie shell

Mix ingredients and fold into the pie shell. Bake at 325 degrees for 1 hour and 5 minutes. This is delicious with vanilla ice cream or whipped cream.

CHOCOLATE CHIP POUND CAKE

1 box yellow cake mix

1 small box vanilla instant pudding

½ cup oil

12 oz. semisweet chocolate chips

1 small box chocolate instant pudding

4 eggs

1-½ cups water

Mix everything but the chocolate chips in a large bowl. Beat for a full 4 minutes with a hand mixer. Fold in the chocolate chips and then pour into a greased bundt pan. Bake 55 minutes at 350 degrees. Let the cake cool in the bundt pan (on a wire rack, if possible) for at least 15 minutes before placing a serving dish over the top of the pan and slowly turning upside down. Tap, tap, tap the bundt pan and slowly remove. Sprinkle the top of the cake with powdered sugar. If you really love your family, you will serve this cake warm with vanilla ice cream. Thank you Tracy Lewis for introducing us to this moist goodness.

CHOCOLATE MERINGUE PIE

- 9-inch deep-dish piecrust
- 1 cup sugar
- ⅓ cup flour
- 2 tablespoons cocoa
- 2 cups milk
- 3 egg yolks, beaten (save whites for meringue)
- Dash salt
- 1 teaspoon vanilla
- 3 tablespoons butter
- Dash cream of tartar
- 6 tablespoons sugar

Bake the piecrust for 10 minutes in a 350-degree oven. Mix the sugar, flour, cocoa, milk, egg yolks and salt. Stir over medium heat until thick, and then add vanilla and butter. Pour chocolate mixture into the pie shell. Top with meringue, spreading all the way to the edges of the crust. Place pie in the oven for 20 minutes or until meringue is brown.

MERINGUE

Use a clean metal or glass bowl. Allow the egg whites to get room temperature. Add a dash of cream of tartar to egg whites and beat with hand mixer until light and fluffy. Slowly add 6 tablespoons of sugar a little at a time and beat some more.

COCONUT CAKE

3 eggs
½ teaspoon vanilla
8 oz. sour cream
⅓ cup water
15-oz. can Coco Lopez® cream of coconut
1 pkg. white cake mix

COCONUT CREAM CHEESE FROSTING

3 tablespoons milk
1 cup coconut flakes
2 cups powdered sugar
1 teaspoon vanilla
1 stick butter, room temperature
8 oz. cream cheese, room temperature

Beat eggs at high speed for 2 minutes. Add sour cream, water, cream of coconut and vanilla, beating well after each addition. Add the cake mix, beating at low until just mixed, then beat at high for 2 minutes. Pour into greased and floured 9" x 13" pan (hold back about ½ cup of the batter or it will outgrow the baking dish when it's baking), and bake at 325 degrees for 45 minutes. Allow cake to cool and place in the freezer for 30 minutes.

Mix the Coconut Cream Cheese Frosting ingredients in a food processor or blender until creamy. Frost the cake and store in the refrigerator. It is best served really cold.

I think we paid a million dollars for Jill Randolph's Famous Coconut Cake at the church auction. It was worth every penny.

COCONUT MERINGUE PIE

- 9-inch deep-dish piecrust
- ⅓ cup sugar
- ⅓ cup flour
- 2 cups milk
- 3 egg yolks, beaten (save whites for meringue)
- Dash salt
- 3 tablespoons butter
- 1 cup coconut
- 1 teaspoon vanilla
- Dash cream of tartar
- 6 tablespoons sugar

Bake the piecrust for 10 minutes in a 350-degree oven. Mix the sugar, flour, milk, egg yolks and salt. Stir over medium heat, stirring constantly, until thick. Add the butter, coconut and vanilla, and stir until combined thoroughly. Add pie mixture to piecrust and top with meringue, spreading to the edges. Sprinkle some coconut on top of the meringue. Bake at 350 degrees for 15 minutes or until meringue is brown.

MERINGUE

Use a clean metal or glass bowl. Allow egg whites to get room temperature. Add a dash of cream of tartar to egg whites and beat with hand mixer until light and fluffy. Slowly add 6 tablespoons of sugar a little at a time and beat some more.

COWBOY COOKIES

2 sticks butter, softened
1 cup sugar
1 teaspoon vanilla
½ teaspoon baking soda
¼ teaspoon baking powder
1-½ cups chocolate chips
⅔ cup shredded coconut

1 cup brown sugar
2 eggs
2 cups flour
½ teaspoon salt
2 cups oats
⅔ cup chopped nuts
⅔ cup raisins

Mix it all up and bake for 15 minutes at 350 degrees. Flatten dough balls a little before baking. These are so stinking good. Best cookie on the planet.

CREAM PIE

1 graham cracker crust
4 bananas, sliced
1 small box instant chocolate pudding (requires milk)
8-oz. tub Cool Whip®

Prepare the chocolate pudding according to the directions on the package. In the graham cracker crust, layer banana slices, prepared pudding and whipped topping. Refrigerate for a couple of hours and sprinkle chocolate shavings on top before serving.

This one is easy and delicious.
Toddlers love to help prepare and eat
this pie on a summer day.

DEPRAVED BROWNIES

17-oz. pkg. chocolate chip cookie mix (requires oil and eggs)
18-oz. pkg. chocolate fudge brownie mix (requires oil and eggs)
14.3-oz pkg. Oreos®

Follow the instructions on the cookie mix package, but add 1 more teaspoon of water and 1 more teaspoon of oil. Spread the cookie dough into the bottom of a greased 9" x 13" glass baking dish. Cover the cookie dough with a layer of Oreos. Follow the instructions on the brownie mix and pour it over the Oreos. Bake for 30 minutes at 350 degrees.

This hot, gooey, delicious mess absolutely begs to be eaten with vanilla ice cream. Be sure to have your insulin nearby.

EASY FUDGE

2 cups semi-sweet chocolate chips (mini chips melt faster)
14-oz. can sweetened condensed milk
1-½ teaspoon vanilla extract
Dash of salt
Dash of cayenne pepper
1 cup pecans, chopped

In a heavy saucepan, over low heat, melt the chocolate chips with the sweetened condensed milk, stirring constantly. Fold in the vanilla, salt and cayenne pepper. Remove from heat and stir in the pecans. Spread evenly into a greased 9" x 9" pan. Chill until firm. Dump onto a cutting board, and cut into squares.

FLOURLESS CHOCOLATE CAKE

2 cups semi-sweet chocolate chips
2 sticks unsalted butter
¼ cup Kahlúa®
8 eggs
¼ cup sugar
1 teaspoon vanilla extract
½ teaspoon salt
Powdered sugar for decoration

Preheat oven to 325. Grease a 9-inch spring-form pan. Line the bottom with parchment paper and then tightly cover bottom and sides with foil and place in a roasting pan. Combine the chocolate chips, butter and Kahlúa in a metal bowl and place the bowl on top of a medium saucepan of boiling water (a makeshift double boiler). Stir until melted and creamy smooth.

Combine eggs, sugar, vanilla and salt in a large bowl and beat with hand mixer for 3 minutes, until frothy. Fold slowly into the chocolate mixture. Pour batter into the spring-form pan and then add enough boiling water to the roasting pan to come halfway up the side of the spring-form pan. Bake at 325 degrees for 30 minutes – until the cake has risen slightly and the edges are just beginning to set. Remove the spring-form pan from the roasting pan and cool on a wire rack to room temperature. Remove foil from spring-form pan and refrigerate overnight.

Remove the spring-form pan from the cake; invert cake onto a larger plate and peel away the parchment paper. Invert again onto serving plate and garnish with powdered sugar.

Debbie Knight is an amazing cook and wonderful human being. She is also going straight to heaven for allowing me to print her coveted Fudge Pie recipe on the next page.

FUDGE PIE

1 stick Imperial® margarine (not butter) 53% vegetable oil spread

1 cup sugar

1 cup chocolate chips

2 eggs

9-inch deep-dish pie shell

Melt margarine in saucepan. Stir in the sugar until completely dissolved into a glassy, thick syrup. Add chocolate chips, stirring constantly until completely melted. Take off the heat and let cool for 10 to 15 minutes, so that eggs won't get scrambled when you mix them into the chocolate mixture. Mix the eggs with chocolate mixture for 4 minutes with hand mixer.

Pour into the pie shell and bake at 350 degrees for 40 minutes.

Pie will rise while cooking and then fall back to normal while it cools. This pie begs to be eaten with a pile of vanilla ice cream.

HELLO DOLLIES

1 stick butter, melted

1-½ cups graham cracker crumbs

2 cups chocolate chips

2 cups coconut

14-oz. can sweetened condensed milk

1 cup pecans, chopped

Combine melted butter with the graham cracker crumbs in a mixing bowl. Press and pack the buttery crumbs into the bottom of a 9" x 13" baking dish. Pour the chocolate chips on top of the graham cracker layer. Next, layer the coconut and then evenly drizzle the can of sweetened condensed milk over the coconut. Evenly distribute the pecans on top of the coconut layer, and bake at 325 degrees for 35 minutes.

KEY LIME PIE

5 egg yolks, beaten
14-oz. can sweetened condensed milk
½ cup key lime juice
9-inch graham cracker crust pie shell

Combine egg yolks with condensed milk and lime juice. Mix well with hand mixer. Pour into graham cracker pie shell. Bake at 375 degrees for 20 minutes. Refrigerate overnight. Top with whipped topping, and garnish with lime slices if desired.

A huge timesaver for this one is to use ½ cup of Nellie & Joe's Famous Key West Lime Juice®. My awesome husband squeezes those tiny key limes by hand.

PEACH COBBLER

1 stick butter

1 cup Bisquick®

1-½ cups sugar (separated)

¾ cup water

2 cups fresh peaches with juice

½ teaspoon cinnamon

½ teaspoon nutmeg

Melt butter in a 9" x 13" baking dish in the oven. Mix the Bisquick, 1 cup of the sugar and water with a hand mixer. Take baking dish out of the oven and pour Bisquick mixture over the melted butter. In a saucepan, combine the peaches, ½ cup sugar, cinnamon and nutmeg, and bring to a boil. Lower heat and simmer until thickened. Pour the peach mixture on top of the batter. Stir with a spoon so that peaches are distributed throughout the batter. Bake at 350 degrees for 60 minutes.

PUMPKIN COFFEE CAKE

2 (16-oz.) pkgs. pound cake mix
2 teaspoons pumpkin pie spice
2 teaspoons baking soda

$2/3$ cup water
15-oz. can solid pack pumpkin
4 eggs

SECRET FILLING

1 cup brown sugar
¾ cup flour

1 cup pecans, chopped
½ cup butter, melted

Combine cake mix, pumpkin pie spice, baking soda, water, pumpkin and eggs in a mixing bowl. Beat well with a hand mixer.

Spread half of the batter into a greased 9" x 13" baking pan. Thoroughly mix the Secret Filling ingredients and distribute evenly on top of the batter. Pour remaining batter on top of the secret filling. Bake at 325 degrees for 55 minutes.

Make blueberry cobbler using Mom's peach cobbler recipe on the prior page by replacing peaches with 3 cups of blueberries and a squeeze of lemon juice.

PUMPKIN PIE

15-oz. can pumpkin

14-oz. can sweetened condensed milk

2 eggs

1 teaspoon cinnamon

½ teaspoon nutmeg

½ teaspoon ginger

½ teaspoon salt

9-inch unbaked deep-dish piecrust

Cool Whip®

Mix all ingredients with hand mixer until smooth. Pour into piecrust. Bake 15 minutes at 425 degrees. Reduce oven heat to 350 degrees and bake for 40 more minutes. Top with Cool Whip.

STRAWBERRY CAKE

1 cup frozen strawberries (thawed)
1 pkg. white cake mix
6-oz. pkg. strawberry gelatin

½ cup cooking oil
4 eggs
½ cup water

MAGIC FROSTING

½ stick butter, room temperature
2 cups powdered sugar

12 oz. cream cheese, room temperature
1 cup frozen strawberries, thawed & drained

Drain and purée the strawberries. Combine all the ingredients with a mixer until smooth. Pour into a greased 9" x 13" glass baking dish and bake at 355 degrees for 38 minutes. Let the cake cool in the refrigerator for an hour or two before frosting. Mix the Magic Frosting in a blender or food processor until it is creamy smooth and then slather on top of the cake. Refrigerate, and prepare to be amazed. We are eternally grateful to Delores Wherry for bringing this slice of heaven into our lives.

Made in the USA
San Bernardino, CA
30 April 2016